# dried

dried

count

count

play

play

seat

seat

magpie

magpie

crayon

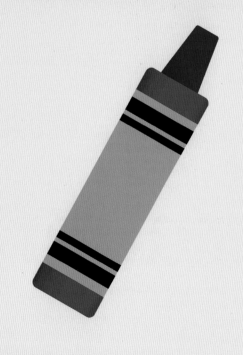

crayon

beak

# beak

cloud

cloud

apple

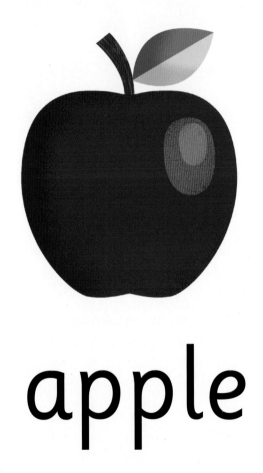

apple

pies

pies

I can see lots of
dark clouds out of
the window today.

Oh no! My tie is
out of reach!

The team felt proud
of their gleaming
silver cup.

I tried to form a little cat out of clay, but it was hard.